a young man
no more

poetry
by

pdmac

Trimble
Hollow
Press

Copyright © 2022

Printed in the United States of America

Published by Trimble Hollow Press

IBSN: 978-0-9915614-8-3

Cover photo and design by Trimble Hollow Concepts

for Terri Lynn
my muse, lover, and best friend

Contents

a young man no more

it's the sigh
folded over this mid afternoon

a slumping limit of edges I cannot touch

I look back at the last hill
and curiously blink in the mottled swirl
of too soon settling sun
my eyes tilted and not sure of how I got here
I remember the road,
yet so much of the view has been cut away

I have become unfamiliar,
a coverless book marked down,
a tombstone beneath the ivy

& I watch them pass
their insolence tossed off
like forgotten clutter
their supple smiles a thin
indictment

I would travel back the way I came
but that road is gone
& the slave at my shoulder
whispers what I knew would happen

I have become my father

walking along the Wannsee

I saw the moon
tonight
& traced your name
along the edges of seas,
dreaming of your face
across this ocean of time

& I smiled
thinking of your day's night
when you see this moon
never knowing
my touch
could reach so far

her

in this cherry blossom morning
I gather up my robe
and wander the pebbled path to my gate
too distracted to notice
I've left the rake by the door

Clayallee corner
(Berlin)

the gray lady
at the bus stop
peers beneath shawls
layered like lazy leaves

her autumn is her slowness
a marionette stiffly moved

yet her brisk eyes
keen with knowing

as she touches my arm
so softly for one so old
her fire like ripe embers
& I smile when she says

"she must be beautiful"

tryst dance

when you left last night
bats whispered among the hedgerows
and fireflies wrote upon the sky

I sat below your window
and watched you undress
marble white
a temple goddess of Corinth

an elder gnome brought wine
and we became drunk
he showed me dances
arm in arm
and called out celtic magic

we laughed when he fell
prone upon the dew
cursing the dawn

he said he loved a woman
like you
alabaster goddess
and taught her dances

he showed me another one
perhaps
when your dreams
abate in the dawn
you would like to learn

schism

you were the perfect Eve
just ever so shy
like midsummer's midnight
standing low and languid
in flesh and books

Nietzsche was so depressing, you said
and I'd agree
never caring for metaphysics
or empiricism
I loved in metaphors

once I compared you
with Galatea:
now I blame you for my fall
something like Icarus
descending

and you became the perfect metaphor
a venus de milo complete
without arms
the ache of your loins
stone within your heart

encounter

how is it
with each autumn
the singing leaves
slip to silence
and alone
or in pairs
gently drift away

the colors I dream
are shrines
and stain-glass reflections
of uncertain lives
spread behind me

and briefly in the wind
a leaf I'd known
almost brown
beside a stone
on my path

a future

autumn is shadows
pulled across afternoons
too early & dim lights
of parlors & kitchens
grabbing an edge
like a corner rug
curling up dusk
into lamp & lilting sky

as a child
I played w/in the tenements
& testaments of those escaped
left letters littered

as if torn pages
of fact or fiction
were enough
to write our future

there were days
high among the chimneys
we would stand
watching autumn set

tugging up woolen hopes
dressed against tomorrow

elves

in this cicada twilight
among the pine song swirl
of ever tree green shadow
comes laughter
lightly wrapped in wind kiss

& I pause
the trace so delicate
I touch my lips to be sure

Uncle Ray's barn

barn loft birds
white dove high
like a Flemish still-life
fly up like white winter wind
around brown baked boards

and the child
an earth below
reaching for feathers freely floating
like copper coins

Concerto for lute

I remember
once in Amsterdam
the lute player
by the shop window
with the night women
and children with streetcar faces
pressed window close
their smiles like mannequins

and the lute player
a beacon beckoning
ballet moths and curios

the children beg coins
and toss innocence
like rings into his case

I see him
tighten his heart left wristed

tonight he will return home
and ponder bodies mostly
and tune his heart in chords
while the women dance

driftwood

the wind beneath the door sings afternoon
a melody of charcoal and brown
like the sky above the sea at Bremerhaven

I walked the beaches once
and though my youth
fled to horizon
carried away by war-horse waves
there was no healing in this sea
and I found none in seagull sky
of aromatic oyster gray

I had sought to release my soul
like a cut albatross
and loft him belly up upon the beach
a gentle corpse friends would recognize
prodding my poems with their toes

there were days the sky showed no emotion
I would sit those hours tight against the door
listening to lines thrown briskly off the shore
haunting hymns within the nets like trapped survivors
bits of lives I heard but never touched

I remember talking to the fisherman
mending nets with the threads of his beard

walk the beach he said
those poems set adrift return
like flotsam bits of broken ships

I found a piece yesterday
and put it on the window ledge
overlooking the garden

and so I promise to come back
buy his beer
and wonder upon what shores
this driftwood would return

looking back

I have taken to fondling photographs
spread like thin wafers of comfort around me

lingering lovingly, longingly
yearning the smoothness of my youth.

I finger the faces that stare at me
often in smiles of shared moment,

the elfin eyes in silent taunt
like an amused anachronism.

My slow hands shuffle memories
like kaleidoscope playing cards,

dealing occasional heartache
from the bottom of the deck.

Later I will stack these gilded stories
like an unkempt journal,

with a profound heaviness,
and a terrible wondering

Canadian requiem

yesterday
with the mist
rising like Gregorian prayer
I listened for the loon
a siren song
beckoning tears

and I heard
his trembling throat
the audible ache of loneliness
like an empty craft
cast adrift

and I spin mid-breath
like geese in flight
anxious for leaving

behind a thousand prayers
mingled with the leaves
wet upon the earth

poems

each man has his own batch of poems
                              -Saul Bellow

descending empty stairways
we sweep the notes
and edges half-rimmed
down one step first
onto another
each act in silhouette
upon the wall

names scratched years before
miming the dull fade
of our trousers

the descent
an unbroken play
with this slow marionette
drifting downstage
amidst the chorus & finale
though quite unlike Ulysses

on the bottom
the broken pile
of violins

chimera

in the silence
between the heartbeats
the wind in black & white
strains against the pillars
and walls of Babylon

and the now deserted ways and alleys
that wind their ways towards darkness

the crenellated words
of spoken thought give way
to the emptiness of tongue
struck dumb this last moment
when the heartbeats stop

& the world is spread in dying embers
like a fire gone cold

Republican exile
(Amsterdam 1981)

he sits next to me
and reads his map through a lens
he says do you speak English
my answer is irrelevant
for he is Portuguese he says
he is a socialist and I think
of Hemingway or Franco
is he a romantic I wonder
is it important
he wants to go downtown
and I see his rosary
his wife is buried downtown
but he has forgotten
how to get to the cemetery
he comes every year
they were married in Andalusia
but he is Portuguese he says
wearing clothes in layers
so cold he must be
his soul-heat numbed to his last ache
of crossing the mountains
she was pregnant he says
but could not keep up
his mouth smiles his hurt
they killed her but he came back
and stole her body
she is buried here now
but he doesn't remember where
Franco was a pig he says
and asks me for a cigarette
as he shuffles to the bus

requiem for an older sister

with your leaving
I close a familiar door
like an Ohio farmhouse
of fine linen memories,
hung outside smells
dappled sun street running slowly
to the river

& the lilacs
beside the church
in the morning

you were there
waiting by the window
like a dog-eared page
I could always find

occasionally
I think of midsummer nights
the years of fireflies
glowing their passion
imprisoned souls
yearning freedom
and a choice
they could not make

sometimes we clung so tightly
the spinning friends
extinguished one by one
immune to hurt or plea

& I remember the river
in raging anger consuming lovers
yet the flowers remained
like so many saints

for Kelsey, my daughter

I watch you in the dappled morning
slip between the grass thin blades
of ambient day & move so gently away
from my hearth

my only daughter
I have loved you with abandon
like a magnificent wind
grown wide

& I listen in the distance
between our voices
for the lilting laughter
of your presence

and the sparrow of your heart
flecked brightly against the sky
sweeping across my day
and tugging at my side

First love

your letters
collect a sun-year's fade

their youth slipping into
yesterday's room
a tacit hush
of discovery and oak
a bookshelf long
stretched between Shakespeare's first sonnet
and Dante's perilous descent,

their voices
now dumbly whisper their supple taunt

remembering the first poem
and its winter birth
our lives ago
your face was lost
in the warm dust
and late afternoon

I have spent my life
growing old

besides
you had your own stories
and other poems

fireflies

they have come for me
this midsummer's night
a rhythmic chorus of siren song
calling me to cut the threads
that bind me to this fate

and so I drift upon their lilting air
when the world is wide and starry
and night folds into night
with the moon hung close
beside the lilacs

and the giddy winds of summer
lift their pulsing promises
lightly beyond my touch
except for this one
captive in my trembling hands

legacy

I have filled my days with emptiness
and gorged my hollow thirst
in the abyss of worthless word

I have become Sisyphus
forever paused
watching what deeds I hold dear
flung to the edges of descent
to slip quietly away

what use is the walk back
or the stone that awaits

what use this limp afternoon
what use this conceited toil

the house I've built
is not my own
neither are the fields I've plowed

for the stranger cups my fertile earth
and pours me into yesterday

I would wrap myself
in woolen hope
had not the birds of prey called out to me

this too is illusion

yet I am compelled
and cannot stop

for my Father
(1922-2003)

upon the ruffled wind
of palm perched ache

I hear your voice
in the ululation
of sun and cloud

and again
in the shimmering pavement
of rolling gently summer

the greens of carefree oaks
stretched thick like nets
upon the day

yet mostly I hear my memory's Mephistopheles
shoulder perched and somber
whispering my one torment

how little have I known you my father

in the repetition of my youth
your music was not my own
your syncopated stories
outside my rhythm

too filled with my own being
I asked too late the harvest songs
of your spring sowing

and now on this sad height
I look behind me
the landscape broad in splendor
I hear your voice again

and again
and again

and I see the fruit of your word
and the cornerstone
so deliberately crafted

raking leaves

in the morning
I am raking leaves

for forty years
I have raked leaves
separating colors into small mounds,
each a mild diversion,
the simultaneous smoke
chewing at my soles,
the smell reminding me
of heavy sweaters.

I laugh my son's name
in liquid breath,
tea steam rising from my teeth.

three mounds ago
I buried my father,
his repose extending east
from the oak in my backfield.

at noon my wife brings me
tea & sweet roll,
now she rests in crimson
at mound one

in the afternoon
I am raking leaves,
aching
my sweater smells of burning leaves,
my hair perfumes the wind

by mid-afternoon
I accept my fate,
like the leaves of my ancestors,
compost for my garden

Class Reunion

in the dusk of my age
I still dream in youth

the supple smile of unfettered ambition
the preening conceit of blithe certainty

the languid creep of looming time
& the quiet fall of insouciant night

& still always in color
the unblemished eyes of blue bright sky

cloud laden hair in disarray
the dandelion wind loft tossed

carelessly adrift
tumbling endlessly behind

like Odysseus pulling up anchor
the waving smile

as she stands on the beach
I won't be long

on the paths beside the Chiemsee
(Prien am Chiemsee)

elf moon
within these phantom trees

a single lamp
upon midsummer's night

& the crocus along
unhurried

Odysseus returning

in parting
we leave rose petals
placing carefully
side to side
dreams and laughter:
waiting
for the sailing ships
and the winded child
crying "they're coming,
they're coming"

in parting

when you left
I saw the wind curled waves
hurled against this empty twilight

& though the plover
skimmed the sky light
in lonely echoed sigh

I felt only the night
like a coal-sacked sound
of cry & wind

on the refusal to mourn a suicide

your illusion grows in pirouettes:
a child martyr for whatever reasons

the tortured petals of distant flowers
trail the grave like a wedding veil,
your metaphor now a closed box

the chimera of his haunting dreams
has wild eyes
and your scented breath
and like Bruegel you dance
the tops of empty tables

I choose to believe your crime
was passion.
thinking it fear,
your revenge is not so sweet

at the Munich Bahnhof

I watch
the old men with envy

their meaning has become trains
& interludes of time
between children
& tea in the afternoons
watching the vineyards
slip into ripples like memory
& dreams of glossy islands
crested with white hopes

thankful for postcards
beyond their touch
& rainbow gold
never found

for Dylan, my son

he climbs into the canyons
of my core, a casual encounter
of the curious.
at six, he has the answer.
a rose, he says, is red.
so simple a truth that it hurts
like watching him sleep
or seeing the nails in His hands

Mid-life pause

across the broad expanse of empty day
I have waylaid my drifting dreams
set down my baggage, so to speak,

& shading my eyes looked out
across the iridescent desert
of tumbleweed encounters

fumbling for words
to slip amongst the lines
of dog-eared chapters

and well-rehearsed fabrications.
what little traffic I have these days
is crammed into well-worn books,

too much to spill at once.
so I wait in the sun mote afternoon
the dust like stories upon my sleeves

too thick to shake off.
& I watch as this day's day
sifts into settled sky

& again into mottled night
more afraid of where I'm going
than where I've been

for I have felt the ruts of my wheels
& the yearning ache of winds
I can no longer touch.

yet tomorrow will I wipe my eyes afresh
carefully nudging brittle pages back into place
& walk once more into the morning

midtown
(Atlanta)

in midtown
there is no church
no stone requiem
of hunched gargoyle granite
with haunting eyes & sinister
smile
just the big-eyed autos
blinking back the grappling
grasp of molasses sweet dark

& we slip amidst
the slender lives of tethered hopes
& shuttered fears
the packaged prudence
of the wander-lost

& walk the streets
upon the windblown scent
of neon sighs

entwined like a vine around an oak
we cloak our touch
like prisoners upon this street
chained to each other

an ending

their church
is soul washed white

the graves orderly
flower trimmed with low hedge
and dirt path

last Friday
they buried an old man
dressed in black

the parish assistant
had raked the paths
painstakingly removing
autumn's leaves

leaving
parallel roads upon the earth

his pride was for the older women
widows who toss roses
upon the dead

and cups of coffee
and gratitude
in warm dull kitchens

and letters from children
too far away

Sailing between Scylla & Charybdis

Who can gauge
What torments rage
Through the whole of me
Gretchen, Goethe's *Faust*

& now do you come to me
unchained Prometheus
your fire's gift dripping searing passion
blackened blaze of madness

I ache within your touch
for I cannot reach righteous reason
pried asunder from ought and want
this willful choice beyond my grasp

& it is you now
the ghost of my soul
perched upon my shoulder
sly mephistopheles
your gift the book of my desire

& cursed am I now
who has found this rainbow gold
in hallowed ground

& I stand amidst the voice & cry
the solemn chants, widsom's reply

yet who has loved as I
this woman so

although apart

& I feel you even now
breast upon chest
supple languid flow of flesh
within flesh
& tightly holding I
press you o so close
wanting the touch
of your beating heart firmly
against my spine

early morning Kyoto

3 lilies
beside the river stone

the path
neatly raked & swirled

& the dragonfly
near your thigh

reverie from Mars Hill

from Mars Hill
the sun drifts on the clouds into Canada,
illuminating a lone auto
fleeing the deepening afternoon

this evening
when I chose to forget
my labors I dreamt
the sun dancing on some hill-spine
as I made my way
through half-picked potato fields

now from Mars Hill
I watch the hurried workers
return, the empty baskets
piled high, the chestnut faces
broad with work's end
and I slip down
into the village past
half-lit homes and neon taverns
the night kaleidoscopes
of secure retreats

nearby, the door
to the congregational church
is carelessly adrift
fanning autumn's wind

and I pause tangled up
in the murmur of hymnal resonance
wondering of the dark auto
this afternoon
and its journey sunward

being in love

from the wind clouds of Olympus
the carrion of battle
descend in triumph

I was near there once
but chose the lesser heights
Cheshire smiling friends
console my pain

it is enough you tried
they say, thankful
I had not
surpassed their dreams

upon the beach

I formed your name upon the beach
kneeling as a priest in solemn ritual
blessing the swirls, the arcs of grace,
the naming of your soul

yet upon the waves
came the wind curled foam
like a flecked stallion hurling the day
upon the sand
and I watched the trembling
rivulets fingering the folds
and valleys of yesterday
and the day before and before
taking sand and sigh
where names slip away
within this autumn tide

some sought the touch
the sacred troth
others fell headlong against the breakers
like wreckage carried high onto the shore

and so I stand watching
the smooth and level sands
blend into sky
and bow in reverent blessing
and trace again the valleys
feeling the skin smooth sand
like a beating heart
and watch the wind and waves
break like brittle glass

denouement

we are inconsistent:

I run memories
like the fleeting miles
of unbroken sorrow

your friends
smile with their lips
and look beyond my shoulder

I arrange and rearrange
photographs and stones
seeking healing in patterns

sometimes I see you
walking
always alone

often I'm window high in dreams
other days I'm a fragile flower
in a vase gone dry

left bank metro
(Paris)

I am with the wind birds
aloft & sunburnt

you walk your streets
in browns
            & urchin clowns
in carnival smile
float amidst the wine & flowers
exaggerated palm
pressing their pity
please

& still
within the metro
the busking songs of winos
echo onto the streets

first born

you contort
so strangely
        asserting
your birthright
as cause
        I don't understand
your anger neither can you
define this plea
for destruction

        & you see
the ache of your father's
liquid eyes
his o so damnable tiredness,
the willingness
        to let
you fall

dear John

you came to me
as the smoke of leaves.

I saw you curl the sky
in half folding both
dusk & fire into lands end

I remembered cresting hills
& flowing down to the river
past your dwelling

& the winter lights
so window bright
pulling night up
like a down comforter

& I came around
the barn then
& found leaves
burnt & blown

so I spread the ashes
still burning like constellations
against a flecked black night

waiting

I waste my days in waiting
an empty wondering wandering
in heartache silence

for I have been here before
the dance all too familiar
the unspoken lines and missed cues
the insipid bravado
the silken vow and distracted pledge

I have been here before
waiting for these winter walls
to fall again into empty vanity

perhaps 'tis better never to have loved

eulogy for an Olympic champion
(for Baron)

the life we ran
was but moments long,
though the pain seemed eternity.
still, you were the victor then
& suffering ebbed with adulation,
hoarse cries, fanfares,
the laurel crown

yet how do the drifting years
regard their champions?
spartan women yielded quicker youth
& our voices became lost
among the queues

even now I watch the gilded youth
sprint beyond our dreams
cresting the clouds of our disbelief

so how is it now
in this autumn twilight
I can only find
your misspelled name in almanacs
wedged among the facts
& baseball players

Cohutta paths
(for Terri)

even now I see her
hovering butterfly high
in this sun entwined morning

her touch like mystic memory
as she draws the soul
from root and fingered prayer

I have shouldered the day's dominion
wrapped in loam and leaf
a fertile planting of expectant footstep

beside the journey
the river sings in colors
a blended harmony of polished stone

beneath the layers of fluid day
I reach in to hold the passing song
and touch a few notes only

yet it is enough
the knowing, the lilt of your voice
with me now, and here

first dance

I sift words in allusion
and bow my intent
in wrapped whisper

cloaked in awkward silence
I proffer a silent gift
hoping this simple rose
would speak

it's the same
each time I see you

the fire behind your eyes
& your dulcet voice
cause me to stumble

& so I stand here in hesitant time
awaiting the sirens' song
unsure of the ropes
that brought me here

juxtaposition

no one sings
through the birds anymore

the locusts drone
layers dust upon mouse bones

the still heat beyond the fields
settles in silence upon the roads

and my mystic father
his voice the hum of summer

gently pointing
to somewhere beyond the swallows

where all time catches up

Memorial Day

though I cannot see
the promise of your day,
I can feel the warmth
of your touch
slipping into the dates
of my journey,
fingering the edges
of my weeping dreams

you, who have no knowing
of my ambition

you are strangers now,
for the familiar ache
of widowed time
has softened
in the winters of memory

& in time
you too will pass
& your sons' daughters will weep
for a time
& you too will be forgotten

like the grass that withers
above my grave
like a field of orchids
bending in a breath of wind

iconic Jesus

pressed between my palms
like thin pages
of romantic novels
this sweet cup
remembers rose and thorn
mingled blood
salty sweat
the skull

my Jesus
hangs iconic
like a hungry Don Quixote

St. Peter's halo
resurrects dust
at his feet

the afternoon sunlight
slips quietly
through crucifix windows
upon plate & chalice
where so lately
porcelain ladies tasted
wine & wafer
in sober reticence

on the wall
Jesus carries adoring lamb

later the men
will come and dust
the hymnal racks

& the cleaning lady
straighten the choir chairs

but when the sun had risen they were
scorched: and because they had no root,
they withered away
                    -Matthew 13:6

tightly
lest like Sisyphus
I lose the stone,
I carry Galilean pebbles:

some I save for altars
some for skimming seas
others below my tongue
for water

at first I could hold
handfuls

now the stone
exceeds my grasp

still-life photo
(on the death of a Kurd and his daughter, 1988)

and still I ache
their dance and bow
in still life
  stretched like a prophet
he offers Ishmael or
is it Isaac or
does it matter his face
is turned away in a way
he hides his doubt
  I will not look
at what is to happen
for by faith are you saved
you and your sons
  and your daughters
  and by faith she fell
at one with her father's hopeless
hurt, yet hoped within
his arms knowing him there
  and like Isaac or
is it Ishmael or
does it matter her gentle head
tilts back as if in wonder
pouting lips asking
why she hurts, why he falls
so tired she is
  and he will rest now
firm in his gift
of a child
who will never
know hunger

combatant

in the autumn of the moon
when swallows and wind
change like flower scent
and the sky closes
its veined fist,
the hammered heart
spins an earth
regardless of dumbness,
pain, or the war
that balances your desire
against my love

For Uncle Ralph
(upon the death of Aunt Anita – Matthew 13:23)

it's the aching of the weeds
taut against my tug,
the slow appraisal of inevitable
yielding in stubborn silence.

I have worked the deep dirt of hope
painfully plucking clean the harried harvest,
and I have measured out the seeds of my seasons
scattering fruit and grain amidst the day.

and I have toiled the furrowed rows
of clod and soil, forcing fences
against their reach.
I blame Adam for these worldly weeds

a curse of wind and sun.
yet here am I harkening to their deeds
acknowledging their game,
the toe over the line faster than I can see.

and now too I grow tired
like Isaac in the autumn,
giving blessings to a future Son

Over the edge

Je suis belle, ô mortels, comme un rêve de pierre,
Et mon sein, où chacun s'est meurtri tour à tour,
Est fait pour inspirer au poète un amour
Éternel et muet ainsi que la matière. *
                    "La Beauté" - Baudelaire

& I feel you even now
the breath upon my spine
brushing the nape-hairs of my reason
curling in the pit of my insanity

& I feel you even now
tongue-tipped dance across my brow
the spirit smoke slipping out of me
my insanity vanishing into eternity

& I feel you even now
the fingerprint upon my chest
layering down through bone and breast
seeking the ember core
of my life's start
your slender soul
wrapped around my heart

I am fair, O mortals, like a dream carved in stone,
And my breast where each one in turn has bruised himself
Is made to inspire in the poet a love
As eternal and silent as matter.

Poets: with a sub-theme in absurdity

do not dream Pegasus
for me, neither sing cathedrals:
no muse, no reeking bards,
no balladeers

my words won't rhyme

I mark the fleeting moments within
your goat-footed smile

I know you don't understand
bronzed smile
all reduced
too absurd

you neither listen nor care

therefore I will hike the streets:
walk where you will.

I will dream the poet
drink the espresso
and watch the metaphors
descend the taverns

untethered

I do not wish
to exchange prisons

my fettered soul
like a leashed falcon
in helpless hooded anger

I count the flowers of my past
an etching of rose upon rose
upon stone
the petals like cuts too deep

yet now you come to me
dancing
a simple rose
pressed between your palms
the moment ebbing my strength

demanding
a piece of my heart
without which
I should not live

walking to the U-Bahn

I see you watching me
through those amber curtains
two floors up
as I slowly walk the city streets

and when our eyes met
you became shadow
a covert lover
pondering

and I turn to appraise sightless manikins
never knowing
the lust in your heart

Anniversary

I still do it
as though looking up
it would matter

your approval

I've grown no beard
nor slippered into reclusive pattering
shuffling to tea
talking of cats
& begging banalities
from morning papers

& I've not found
trousers creased by corner closets
or shirts of age grown small

nor do I sit
with the pandering of old men
beached by wives
& recipes & routines
of scattering photos
and loneliness like pigeon feed

rather now have I grown
interlocked pieces fitting into sky
earth-blown and evergreen
blending just so
finding all the edges first

& still I arise
knowing today
I'll again
not see you

www.ingramcontent.com/pod-product-compliance
Lightning Source LLC
Chambersburg PA
CBHW060352050426
42449CB00011B/2950